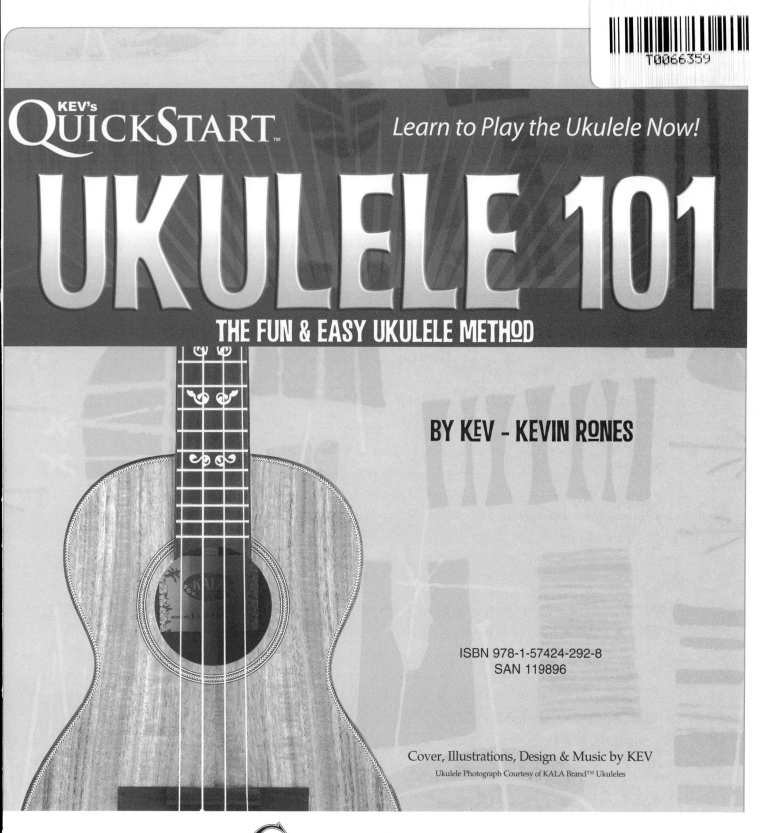

KEV's QUICKSTART™

Learn to Play the Ukulele Now!

UKULELE 101

THE FUN & EASY UKULELE METHOD

BY KEV - KEVIN RONES

ISBN 978-1-57424-292-8
SAN 119896

Cover, Illustrations, Design & Music by KEV
Ukulele Photograph Courtesy of KALA Brand™ Ukuleles

Copyright © 2013 CENTERSTREAM Publishing, LLC
P.O. Box 17878 - Anaheim Hills, CA 92817

www.centerstream-usa.com

TABLE OF CONTENTS

KEV's Quickstart™ Companion CD Track List

WELCOME TO
UKULELE 101

This book was designed as an introduction into the world of the Ukulele.

With the method presented in this book you should gain a basic understanding of the ukulele and amaze and impress your friends and family with your new knowledge and playing abilities!

Many of the Exersongs™ in this book are done in Tablature and Standard Music Notation with Chords so you can practice strumming, or play the melody and picking patterns along with the CD.

UKE can do it!

PLAY UKULELE
IT'S FUN AND
REALLY GOOD
FOR YOU.

KNOWING YOUR UKULELE

What type of Ukulele do you play?

Ukuleles come in all shapes, designs, colors and sizes. They can be put into two categories:

Novelty and Souvenirs Ukuleles
This includes ukuleles with unusual shapes, ukuleles created as advertising promotions, movie, theater and show props, gimmicks and decoration.

Player Ukuleles
Ukuleles designed to create music. These can be divided into four basic sizes: Soprano, Concert, Tenor and Baritone.

The Four Basic Ukulele Sizes

SOPRANO
Size: 20" *
Fretboard Length (scale):13.5"
Frets: 12-15*

Tuning
G C E A

CONCERT
Size: 24" *
Fretboard Length (scale):15"
Frets: 15-17*

Tuning
G C E A

TENOR
Size: 26" *
Fretboard Length (scale):17"
Frets: 18-20*

Tuning
G C E A

BARITONE
Size: 30" *
Fretboard Length (scale):19"
Frets: 19-20*

Tuning
D G B E

* Length and fret numbers can vary between ukulele builders.

Soprano
The Soprano or Standard size ukulele is the smallest and most widely owned ukulele. These ukuleles are very portable and are usually the least expensive, producing the higher "treble" sound commonly associated with the ukulele. Soprano sized ukuleles are usually tuned in standard C (High G) tuning.

Concert
Concert ukuleles are sometimes referred to as the Alto Ukulele. They are little larger than the Sopranos with a slightly fuller sound. Concert Ukuleles have a higher string tension and wider frets. There can be up to 20 frets on a Concert Ukulele. Concert sized ukuleles are usually tuned in standard C (High G) tuning, however some people prefer C (Low G) tuning in which the G string is tuned down an octave.

Tenor
Tenor ukuleles are larger than Concert sized ukuleles. Because of their rich full sound, and additional frets the Tenor is the popular choice for fingerstyle ukulele enthusiasts. Tenor sized ukuleles are usually tuned in standard C (High G) tuning, however some people prefer C (Low G) tuning in which the G string is tuned down an octave. Tenor Ukuleles are sometimes tuned lower like a Baritone ukulele.

Baritone
The Baritone ukulele is a little bigger than the Tenor sized ukuleles. It is tuned exactly like the top four strings on a guitar. D G B E. It is sometimes referred to as "the little guitar". Because the strings on a Baritone are tuned 4-half steps lower the Chord names are different than the Soprano, Concert and Tenor ukuleles.

UKULELE HISTORY

It's always good to know a little a little history about the ukulele. When people see you playing one they often ask about the instrument. Be prepared with a brilliant response!

A Brief History Of The Ukulele

The Ukulele (pronounced oo • koo • lay • lay) is best known for its association with the great musical tradition of the Hawaiian Islands. It was developed in the 1800's by Portuguese immigrants who delighted the Hawaiians with street performances on small 4-string guitar like instruments called *cavaquinhos* (pronounced kaw • va • keen • yo).

The ukulele was established in Hawaiian music largely due to the support and promotion of the instrument by King David Kal'kaua (1836 -1891). He was a patron of the Arts sometimes known as the *Merrie Monarch*. He included the ukulele in many performances and royal gatherings.

Queen Lili'uokalanii, the last Hawaiian Monarch (1891-1893) taught that the word *Ukulele* means "The gift that came here", and was based from the Hawaiian words *uku* (reward or gift) and *lele* (to come). Others say that the name means *Jumping Flea*- describing the way the fingers move on the ukulele fretboard.

In 1915 the Ukulele was showcased at the *Panama Pacific Exposition* in San Francisco. Its popularity with visitors caused a fad for Hawiian-themed music and helped to introduce the ukulele to the world. Soon the ukulele was adopted by vaudeville performers and jazz musicians throughout the mainland.

Roy Smeck "The Wizard of the Strings"

Roy Smeck (1900-1994) was one of the original innovators on the ukulele. He started his career on the vaudeville circuit. Knowing he could not sing well, he developed his skills on guitar, banjo and ukulele and added trick playing and novelty dances to his act.

Roy was dubbed "The Wizard of the Strings" and was one of the first to incorporate fingerstyle, tapping and percussive techniques on the ukulele.

He made over 500 recordings and wrote instructional method books and arrangements for the instruments he played. Smeck invented and endorsed the Vita-Uke and other stringed instruments. In 1926 Warner Brothers released the film *Don Juan* starring John Barrymore. It was the first feature film using the new Vitaphone sound-on-disc system. The preview to that film was a short film featuring Roy Smeck titled *His Pastimes* which made him an instant celebrity.

STRING NAMES AND NUMBERS

String Names: **G C E A**

String Numbers: 4 3 2 1

An easy way to remember the string names is the mnemonic:

Good **C**ows **E**at **A** lot

Standard Ukulele Tuning

The strings are pitched to the most common Ukulele tuning for Soprano, Concert (Alto) and Tenor ukulele. It is also referred to as "*C tuning*" (G C E A) .

The two preferred ways to string a Ukulele

If you go to a music store to buy a set of ukulele strings they will ask you if you want a **High G** or a **Low G** set. The only difference between the two string sets is one uses a deeper sounding heavier gauge G (4th) string.

Which string set should you buy?

Both types of string sets are acceptable. Most people prefer using High G strings.

Standard C with a high G string
This is the most widely used ukulele tuning and gives the ukulele its singularly recognizable sound. It is sometimes referred to as Standard or reentrant tuning.

Standard C with a low G string
This tuning is similar to a guitar tuning. It is sometimes preferred for Jazz and Classical ukulele music because it offers access to lower pitched notes.

Reentrant tuning is just a fancy way to say that the instrument is strung with strings that are not ordered from the lowest pitch to highest pitch. The Five-String Banjo and the Sitar are examples of other instruments that have *reentrant tuning*.

3 **C** — **E**

4 **G** — **A**

G C E A
4 3 2 1

INSIDE
String Set

OUTSIDE
String Set

How is your Ukulele strung?

Standard C with a high G string
If your G (4th) string is a thinner gauge than your C (3rd) string your ukulele is set up to play in Standard C tuning with a High G.

Standard C with a low G string
If your G (4th) string is a thicker gauge than the other strings your ukulele is strung in Standard C tuning with a Low G.

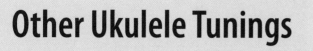

Other Ukulele Tunings

While this book focuses mainly on *Standard Ukulele tuning* it is important to note that there are other tunings used on the ukulele.

Baritone Ukulele Tuning (D, G, B, E)

This tuning is sometimes referred to as "G tuning." It is tuned the same as the last four strings on a guitar and is used on baritone ukuleles and less frequently on the tenor ukulele.

Slack-key Tuning (G, C, E, G)

This tuning is almost identical to **Standard Ukulele Tuning** (G, C, E, A) with one exception, the 1st (A) string is tuned higher to a G note. This is called an *Open Tuning* because when you strum the open strings (not fretting any notes) it makes a C major chord. *Slack-Key Tuning* is played in both **Low** or **High G**.

English Tuning (high A, D, F#, B)

This tuning is sometimes called *D Tuning*. The only difference between this tuning and *Standard C tuning* is each string is one whole step higher in pitch.

*M*uch of the early vintage ukulele music was written in *English D Tuning* however In the early 1900's ukulele method books were published using the more musically friendly *C tuning*, which was easier to teach. Eventually *C tuning* became more widely used and accepted as the standard tuning for Soprano, Concert and Tenor Ukulele.

Canadian Tuning (low A, D, F#, B)

This tuning is nearly identical to *English D tuning* except it uses a low **A** string. Even though this tuning is less frequently used It is still being taught in some Canadian ukulele programs and is sometimes referred to as *Canadian Tuning.*

PARTS OF THE UKULELE

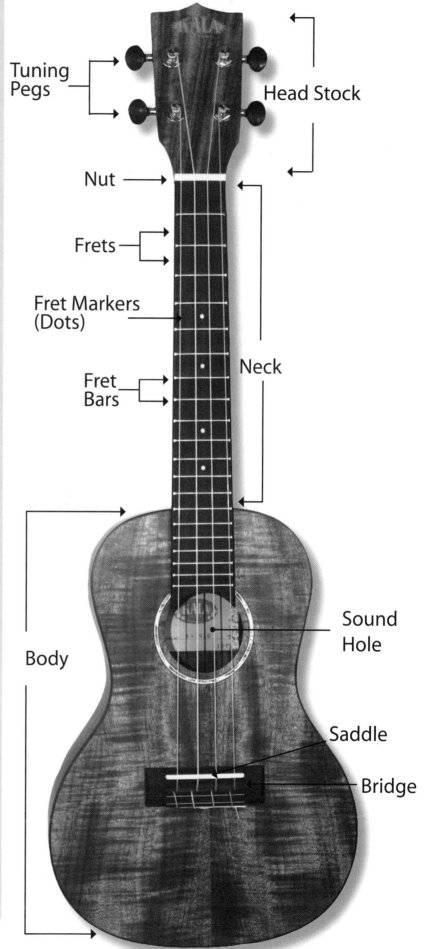

Tuning Pegs

Head Stock

Nut

Frets

Fret Markers (Dots)

Neck

Fret Bars

Sound Hole

Body

Saddle

Bridge

TUNING YOUR UKULELE

C tuning (High G) - G C E A

Tuning to a Piano

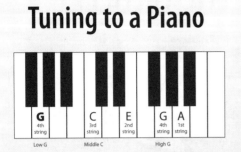

Standard C (High G)

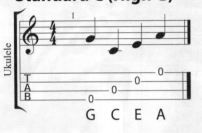

G C E A

Standard C (Low G)

G C E A

Other Tuning Devices

The process of finding the correct pitch for each string and becoming familiar with the sound of a perfectly tuned strings is a great way to train your ear.

There are a number of inexpensive electronic tuners on the market.

Digital Contact Tuners - These tuners clip directly onto the headstock of your instrument. They pick up the vibration of your strings and display the note your string is playing.

Smart Phone Apps - If you have a smart phone you can download many free Ukulele Tuner apps.

Free On-line tuners- If you have internet access you can find free on-line tuners.

How often should you tune your ukulele?
Before you begin playing you should *always* tune your ukulele!

How Tune Your Ukulele Using Relative Tuning

If you don't have access to a tuner you can still tune the ukulele to itself. This method of tuning is called *Relative Tuning*. *With this method your ukulele may not be in pitch to play with other instruments.*

Step 1. Tighten the **C** (3rd) string until you feel it sounds in pitch.

Tune the **E** (2nd) string

Step 2. Press your left index finger onto the fourth fret of the **C** string of your ukulele. This is an **E** note. Play the **E** note on the **C** string and then strike the open **E** string. Turn the **E** string until the notes of both strings sound the same.

Tune the **A** (1st) string

Step 3. Press your left index finger onto the fifth fret of the 2nd **E** string of your ukulele. This is an **A** note. Play the **A** note on the **E** string and then strike the open **A** (2nd) string. Turn the first string **A** until both strings sound the same.

Tune the High **G** (4th) string

Step 4. Press your left index finger on the third fret of the **E** (2nd) string of your ukulele. This is a **G** note. Play the **G** note on the **E** (2nd) string and then strike the open **G** (4th) string. Both strings should sound the same. Turn the **G** (4th) string until both strings sound the same.

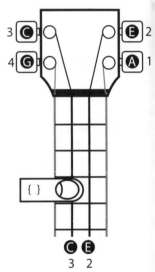

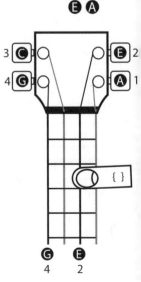

HOW TO HOLD THE UKULELE

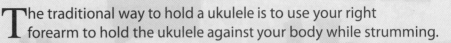

The traditional way to hold a ukulele is to use your right forearm to hold the ukulele against your body while strumming.

People and ukuleles come in a variety of different shapes and sizes. Adjust your instrument so your hand falls over the sound hole while strumming.

Some people prefer to use a *ukulele strap*. A properly adjusted ukulele strap will help you keep your instrument in proper playing position while standing or sitting and allow for easier finger picking technique.

KEEP YOUR INSTRUMENT'S NECK AT A COMFORTABLE UPWARD ANGLE.

REMEMBER PRACTICE MAKES PERMANENT!

*If you practice playing badly, you will be **REALLY good** at **PLAYING BADLY**. Use good form everytime you practice and your playing will improve quicker!*

Using a Ukulele Strap

There are many types of ukulele straps on the market. Some hook in the sound hole from underneath offering little stability. Others are tied on. The best way is to use **Strap Buttons** as shown in the photos. These can be easily installed on your ukulele. Your local music store can usually do it for you. Get a nice comfortable strap and you're ready to gig!

Strap Buttons

WARNING! if you have a rare or vintage ukulele consult with a professional BEFORE modifying your instrument.

BASIC STRUMMING 101

There are several ways to strum the ukulele. For the purposes of this book we will use the two most common strum techniques. **The Index Brush Strum** is one of the most common ukulele strumming techniques. We'll be using the Index Brush Strum as our basic "Go To" strum to build our strumming fundamentals.

Basic Index Brush Strum

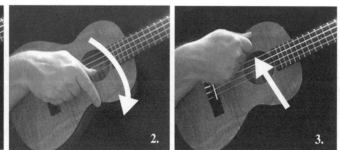

Use the cookie crumb technique!

Think of the down stroke as the same motion you would use to gently brush cookie crumbs off your favorite shirt.

1. Start the strum by forming a loose fist and turn your palm slightly upward so you can see your fingernails. *Push your elbow forward until the nail of your index finger is aligned to the strings.*

2. Strum downward using the back of your fingernail at an approximate 90 degree angle to the strings. *Pivot from your elbow using a movement similar to the motion of a windshield wiper blade*

3. On the downstroke let your fingers fall open naturally. *The index finger is mostly used for the strum, however some players also choose to allow the middle and third finger to make contact with the strings.*

Alternating Index Brush & Thumb Strum

1. Start with the Basic Index Strum.
2. As your index finger reaches the bottom arc of the strum turn your wrist and align the nail of your thumb to the strings. *This is similar to the motion of checking the time on a wrist watch.*
3. Strum up with your thumb using a *"Thumbs up"* motion.

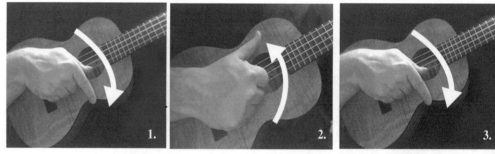

This strum is similar to the motion you would make if you were rolling dice to the ground.

STRUMMING NOTES*

THE STRUM ZONE

Before you learn to play chords on the ukulele it's a good idea to get your groove on. Adding chords will slow you down and cause your timing to be off. Learn a basic strum using the open strings and practice keeping a beat. *Remember to tap your feet and stay in rhythm!* When you're ready, add in some new chord changes.

You can mute (muffle) the strings by lightly covering them with your fretting hand to deaden the string while strumming.

Where to strum. Everyone is a different size. Ukuleles also come in different sizes. Some people strum over the frets while others strum over the sound hole. You can get different tones by strumming over the sound hole or closer to the bridge. Master the Strum Zone. Try them all!

BASIC SLASH RHYTHM

Basic SLASH marks are sometimes used to indicate how many BEATS are available in each measure. In this example the slashes indicate *4 beats per measure*. You can use different rhythms and strumming patterns that fit the style of the music as long as they can fit into 4 beats of music.

Chord Names or Chord Diagrams are above the slash indicating the chord to play and when to change it.

No chord above a measure? Keep playing the C chord until the next chord comes up!

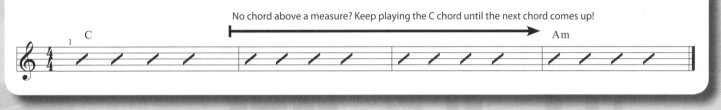

 Track 02

TWO STRUMMING PATTERNS

Here are 2 basic "Go To" strumming patterns shown in relation to a basic slash rhythm.
D = Downward Strum (downstroke) **U** = Upward Strum (upstroke)

Strum 01: Quarter Note Strum

Strum 02: Basic Strum

COUNTING 4/4 TIME

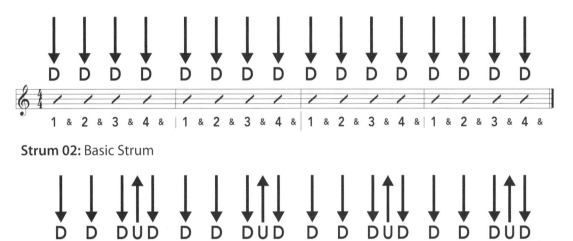

13

READING A CHORD DIAGRAM

A chord diagram is a graphical representation of the ukulele fretboard from the same perspective that you would view your ukulele if it were on a stand in front of you.

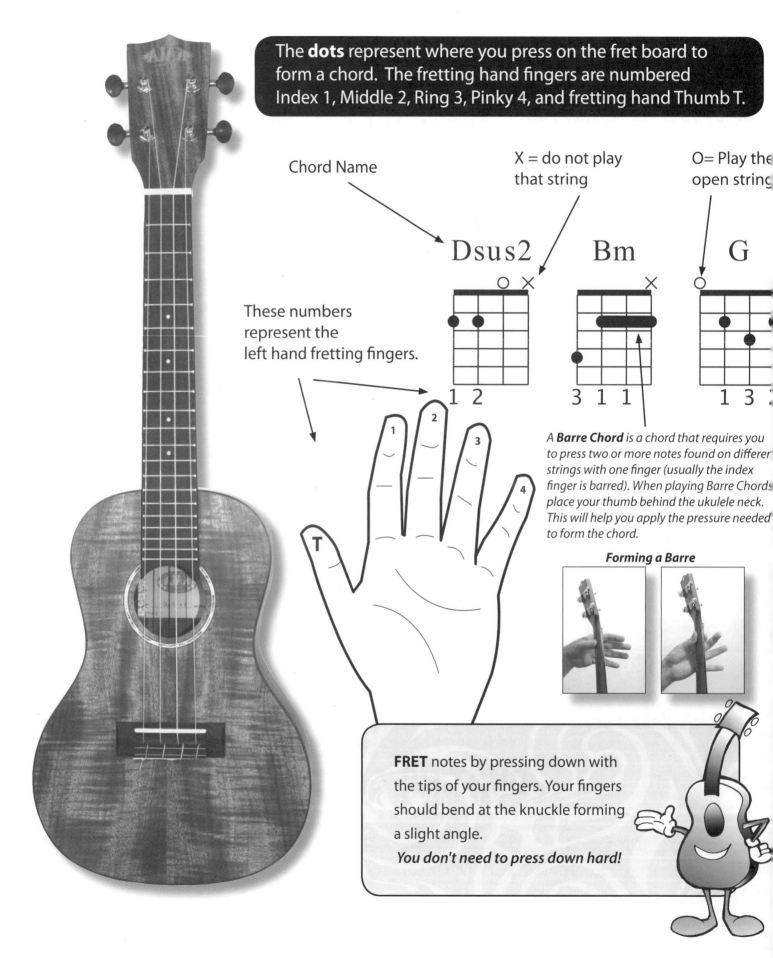

The **dots** represent where you press on the fret board to form a chord. The fretting hand fingers are numbered Index 1, Middle 2, Ring 3, Pinky 4, and fretting hand Thumb T.

Chord Name

X = do not play that string

O= Play the open string

These numbers represent the left hand fretting fingers.

Dsus2   Bm   G

1 2   3 1 1   1 3

A **Barre Chord** is a chord that requires you to press two or more notes found on different strings with one finger (usually the index finger is barred). When playing Barre Chords place your thumb behind the ukulele neck. This will help you apply the pressure needed to form the chord.

Forming a Barre

FRET notes by pressing down with the tips of your fingers. Your fingers should bend at the knuckle forming a slight angle.
You don't need to press down hard!

LEARNING YOUR FIRST CHORDS

Practice these chords using strumming patterns 01 and 02 (see page 13).

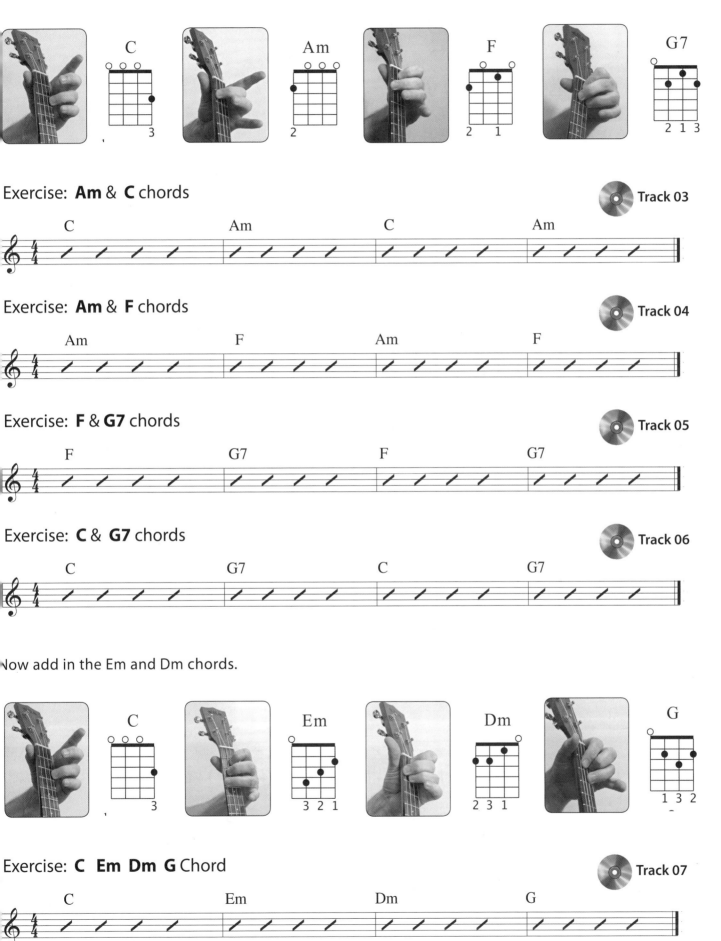

Exercise: **Am** & **C** chords ●)) Track 03

Exercise: **Am** & **F** chords ●)) Track 04

Exercise: **F** & **G7** chords ●)) Track 05

Exercise: **C** & **G7** chords ●)) Track 06

Now add in the Em and Dm chords.

Exercise: **C Em Dm G** Chord ●)) Track 07

PROGRESSIONS USED IN A ZILLION TUNES!

A **CHORD PROGRESSION** is a group of chords played in a sequence. Often one progression is used for the **VERSE** of a song and another for the **CHORUS** or **BRIDGE**. Many songs use the same chord progressions played in different tempos and KEYS.

The Doo Wop Progression (I vi IV V7)

This progression was used in many songs of the 50's and 60's like *Blue Moon* and *Earth Angel* by the Penguins.

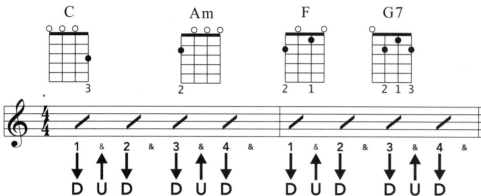

Track 08

The Pop Reggae Progression (I V vi IV)

This progression has an upbeat Reggae feel similar to the style of Jason Mraz's hit *I'm Yours*.

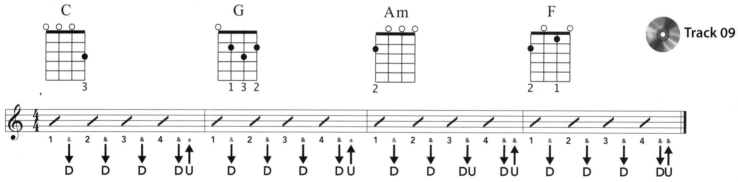

Track 09

The "Stand by Me" Progression (I vi IV V7 I)

This progression was used in classic songs like *Stand By Me* by Ben E. King.

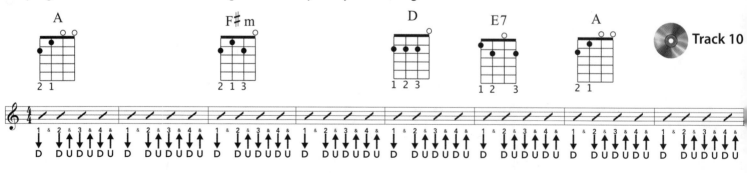

Track 10

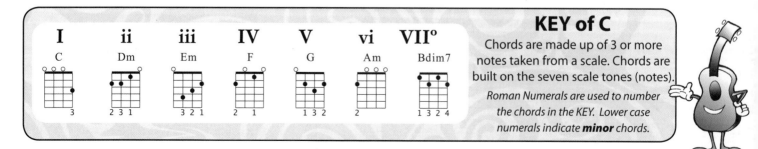

I	ii	iii	IV	V	vi	VII°
C	Dm	Em	F	G	Am	Bdim7

KEY of C

Chords are made up of 3 or more notes taken from a scale. Chords are built on the seven scale tones (notes).

*Roman Numerals are used to number the chords in the KEY. Lower case numerals indicate **minor** chords.*

60's Rock & Roll Progression (I IV V7)

This progression was used in hit songs like *Twist and Shout* by the Beatles and *La Bamba* by Richie Valens.

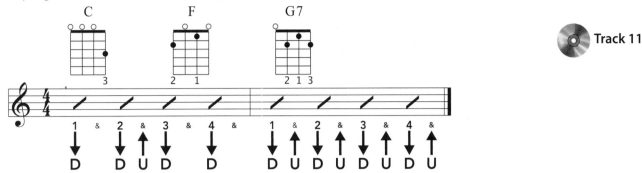

 Track 11

The "Louie Louie" Progression (I IV V)

This progression was used in hit songs like *Louie Louie* by the Kingsmen and *Wild Thing* by the Troggs.

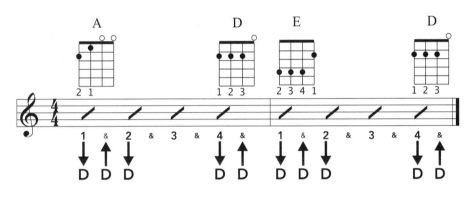

Track 12

The "Knocking on Heaven" Progression (I IV ii)

This progression was used in hit songs like Bob Dylan's *Knockin on Heaven's Door*.

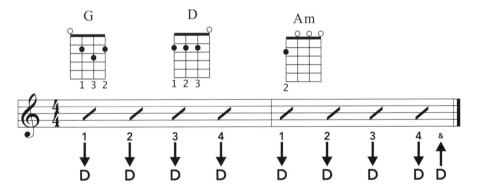

Track 13

The "Sweet Home" Progression (I IV V)

This progression was used in hit songs like Lynryd Skynyrd's *Sweet Home Alabama* and Warren Zevon's *Werewolves of London*.

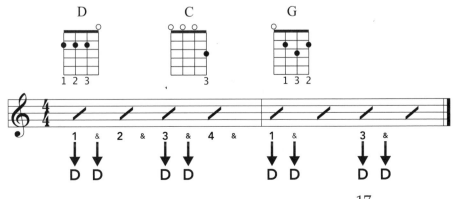

 Track 14

YOU CAN'T SHINE UNLESS YOU TWINKLE FIRST
LEARN THIS TUNE... YOU'RE GOING TO NEED IT!

TWINKLE

```
C        /       F   C
Twin-kle, twin-kle lit-tle star,
F     C      G      C
How I won-der what you are.
C    F      C     G
Up a-bove the world so high,
C    F        C    G
Like a dia-mond in the sky.
C        /       F   C
Twin-kle, twin-kle lit-tle star,
F     C      G      C
How I won-der what you are.
```

BONUS!

TWINKLE USES EXACTLY THE SAME CHORDS & STRUMS AS THE ALPHABET SONG

A slash mark / tells you to strum the preceeding chord again.

Alphabet Song

```
C        /        F      C
a - b - c - d - e - f - g
F        C    G          C
h - i - j - k - l - m - n - o - p
C     F        C     G
q - r - s and - t - u - v
      C    F       C       G
(w) double-you and - x - y - z
C        /        F   C
Now I  know  my  A-B-C's
F         C        G       C
Next - time won't you sing with me?
```

Many ukulele groups have song sheets in this format.

Reference *Chord Diagrams* are sometimes pictured on the song sheet with the *Chord Names* shown above the lyrics.

Home On The Range

```
        C                          F
Oh, give me a home where the buff-a-lo roam,
        C                   G7
Where the deer and the antelope play;
        C                         F
Where seldom is heard a dis-cour-aging
Fm          C        G7        C
word, and the skies are not cloud-y all day.
```

(Chorus)

```
C      G7        C
Home,  home on the range,
                   D7          G7
Where the deer and the an-te-lope play;
        C                      F         Fm
Where seldom is heard a dis-cour-ag-ing word,
        C        G7      C
and the skies are not cloud-y all day.
```

CHORDS IN KEYS

KEY of C

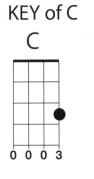 C
0 0 0 3

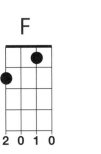 F
2 0 1 0

 G7
0 2 1 3

Key of Am

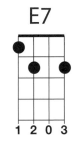 Am
2 0 0 0

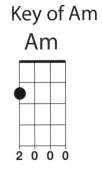 Dm
2 3 1 0

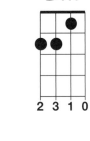 E7
1 2 0 3

KEY of G

 G
0 1 3 2

 C
0 0 0 3

 D7
1 1 1 3

Key of Em

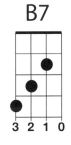 Em
0 3 2 1

 Am
2 0 0 0

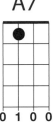 B7
3 2 1 0

KEY of F

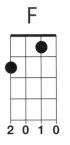 F
2 0 1 0

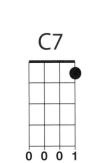 B♭
3 2 1 1

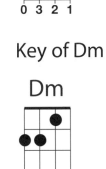 C7
0 0 0 1

Key of Dm

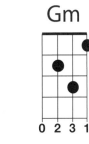 Dm
2 3 1 0

 Gm
0 2 3 1

A7
0 1 0 0

KEY of D

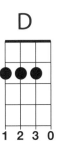 D
1 2 3 0

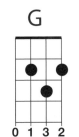 G
0 1 3 2

A7
0 1 0 0

Key of Bm

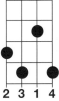 Bm
3 1 1 1

Em
0 3 2 1

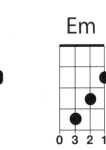 F♯7
2 3 1 4

KEY of Bb

 B♭
3 2 1 1

E♭
2 3 4 1

F7
2 3 1 4

Key of Gm

Gm
0 2 3 1

Cm
0 3 3 3

 D7
1 1 1 3

© 2013 KEV-Kevin Rones, Kev's QuickStart™ www.KEVmusic.com

HOW TO READ TABLATURE

It's easy!

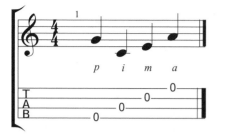

The exercises in this book are written in both *Standard Music Notation* and *Ukulele Tablature.*

The diagram on the left shows the open strings of the Ukulele in *Standard Music notation* (top) and *Tablature* or *TAB* (bottom). The lower case letters *p i m a* refer to the right hand fingers.

Tablature or *TAB* is system of music notation that tells you which string and fret to play. Each of the four staff lines represent a string on the ukulele. The numbers on each line (string) indicate which fret to press as the string is played.

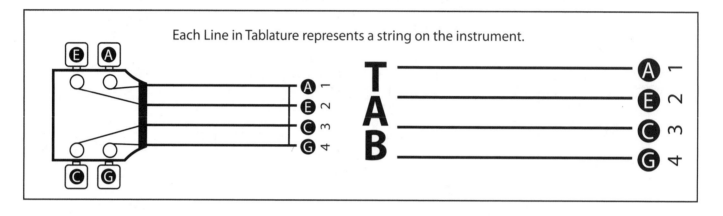

Each Line in Tablature represents a string on the instrument.

 Track 17

Reading your first notes in TAB

The numbers on the lines indicate which fret to press on that string. In the example to the right we see the number 3 indicated on the A string. Press your finger on the third fret of the A string and play that note.

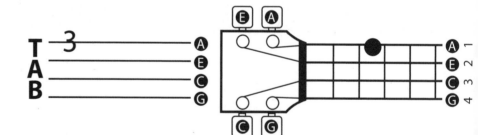

In TAB a zero on any line means you play the open (unfretted) string.

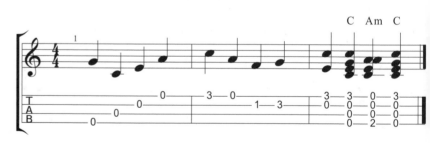

As is in classical music notation (above), we read TAB from left to right and use the vertical bars to organize the TAB notes into spaces called measures. When two or more numbers are stacked on top of each other those notes are played at the same time. Often chord names or diagrams are shown above TAB notes. **Remember: Play only the notes indicated in the TAB.**

Here are some basic techniques that are used in the songs and exercises in this book.

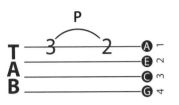

The Pull-off Track 18

Place your 2nd finger (middle) on the third fret and your first finger on the second fret of the **A** (1st) string. Strike the **A** string and pull your 2nd finger (middle) off the string to create the second note. Strike the string one time only!

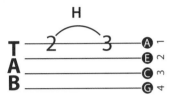

The Hammer-on  Track 19

Place your 1st finger (index) on the second fret of the **A** (1st) string. Strike the **A** string and "hammer" your 2nd finger (middle) on the third fret to play the second note. Strike the string one time only!

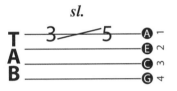

The Slide  Track 20

Place your 3rd finger (annular or ring finger) on the third fret of the **A** (1st) string. Strike the **A** string, press down on the fret and *slide your finger* from the 3rd to the 5th fret.

Exercise: Get down on some Blues

In this exercise play the *Pull-off*, *Hammer-on* and *Slide* techniques as indicated. Notice how similar the notation for each technique is when comparing *Standard Music Notation* with *Tablature*.

New to reading TAB?
Listen to the companion Track 07 for a step-by-step explanation of this exercise.

Track 21 Step-By-Step

Track 22

Riffin' the Blues
Pull-offs, Hammer-ons & Slides

This Exersong™ is based on a very fast Traditional French song used for a riotous dance called the Can-Can.

Track 23

The Can-Can
Traditional French Song

Arranged by KEV

This Exersong™ is based on the Brazilian choro music piece *Tico-Tico no Fubá* composed by Zequinha de Abreu. It translates to *Little Sparrow in the Flour.*

Track 24

Tico Tico
Brazilian Choro Music

Arranged by KEV

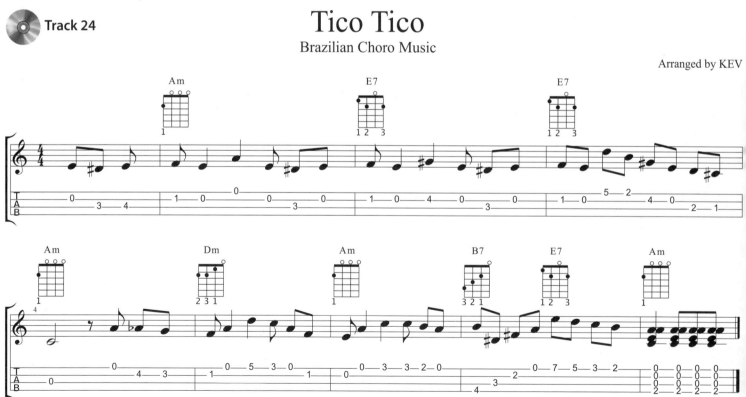

22

This Exersong™ has several chord changes. Practice the melody and chords with the CD. One strum per chord.

Track 25

America The Beautiful
Music by Samuel A. Ward

Arranged by KEV

WHAT THE HECK IS A HAWIIAN D7?

Many Hawiian songs use an easy to play two finger D7 Chord that has a more mellow tone than the standard D7 barre chord. It's really a D7 with no root note (D).

D7

Track 26

Ah! Vous dirai-je, maman
French Folk Song

Arranged by KEV

Track 27

El Bamba
In the Style of Richie Valens

Track 28

A Little Black Dog
In the style Jimmy Page

Track 29

COUNTING 3/4 TIME

KEV's
QuickStart
Uke

Für Elise
Ludwig van Beethoven

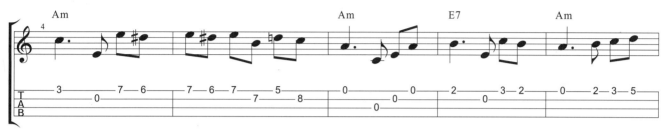

Track 31

Minuet in G
J.S. Bach

Practice the melody for this Exersong™ with the CD and then practice the chord progression using the strumming pattern at the bottom of the song.

Track 32

The Meadow

Music by KEV-Kevin Rones

Each measure in this piece gets three beats.
It is counted 1 - 2 & 3. Down Down UP Down

A Calliope is a very loud steam-powered organ historically used for carousels at traveling circuses. It played music that followed the rhythm of the up and down motion of the carousel horses. Try playing the chords along with the CD using the strumming pattern below.

Track 33

Music For a Lost Calliope

Music by KEV-Kevin Rones

Each measure in this piece gets three beats.
The first beat is not played.
REST - 2 - 3 REST - 2 - 3 REST - 2 - 3

FINGER PICKING 101

KEV's
QUICKSTART
UKE

WONDERING WHICH FINGERS TO PICK WITH?

INTRODUCING THE FABULOUS FINGER FINDING NOTATION SYSTEM...

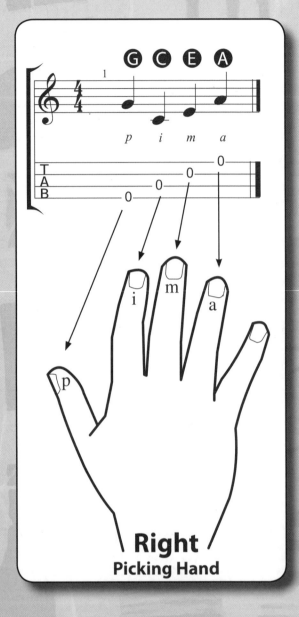

Right
Picking Hand

p i m a

Since we do music notation for both the strumming or **PICKING** hand and the **FRETTING** hand we need a way to differentiate between them.

p i m a notation is used to indicate which *picking hand fingers* to use. It is most commonly associated with the Spanish names for the fingers. It is noted in lower case letters and found next to the note or below the music staff in both Tablature and Standard musical notation.

p = pulgar (thumb)
i = indice (index)
m = medio (middle)
a = anular (ring)

What about the little finger?
We almost never use it for fingerpicking.
It is sometimes referred to as X, C or E depending on the style of music played.
For the purposes of this book we will call it the *stinky pinky* and ignore it.

This example uses the same right hand picking pattern as the hand illustration above. Try playing it a few times then apply it to the chord changes in Canon in C.

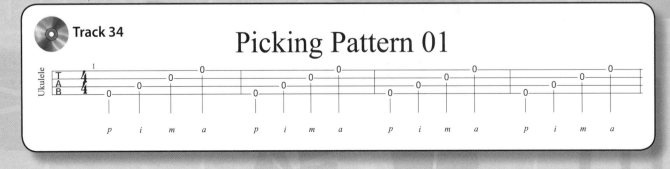

Track 34

Picking Pattern 01

This Exersong™ was adapted from sections of Pachelbell's Canon in D. There are two ukulele parts. The top *Staff and TAB* show the melody or *lead* part. The bottom TAB line shows the *Picking Pattern Accompaniment.* Simply play the chord progression and use **Picking Pattern 01**. Then play the melody with the CD backing track.

Canon in C
Adapted from Johann Pachelbel's Canon in D

Arranged by KEV

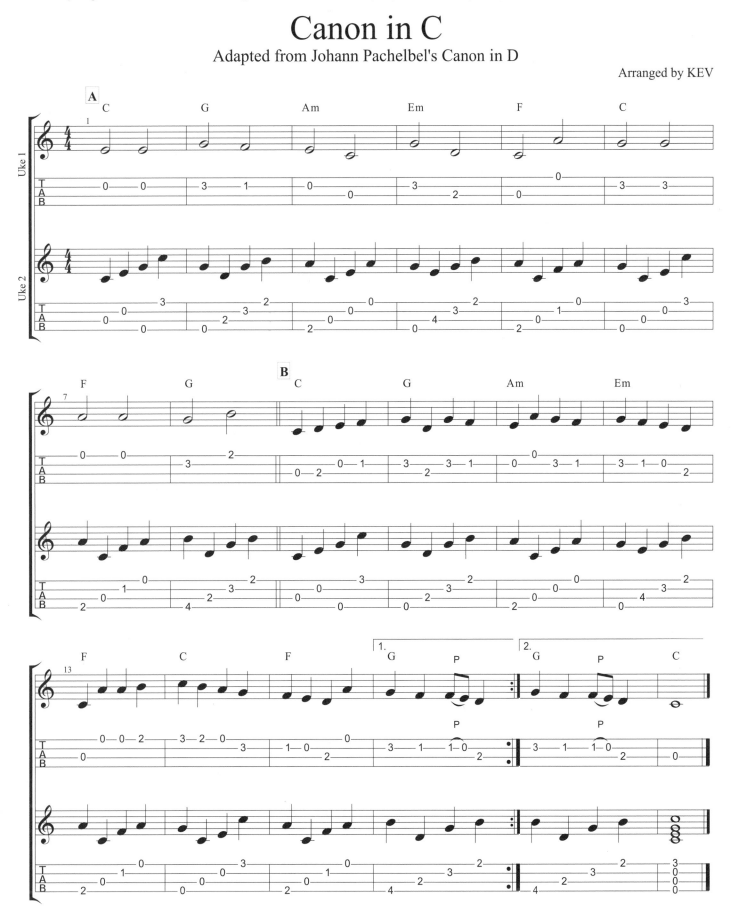

LET'S GET PICKING!

Start by playing Picking Pattern 02 without fretting any notes. Use the *pima system* to get your right hand picking correctly.

Play the pattern until you develop good muscle memory. When you can play it easily try playing the Exersong™ Blues It.

Use your Knowlege to Build Your Skills

Once you can play a picking pattern you can use it in many chord progressions. Go back to page 16 and try each of the four picking patterns on the progressions you learned earlier.

Track 36

Picking Pattern 02

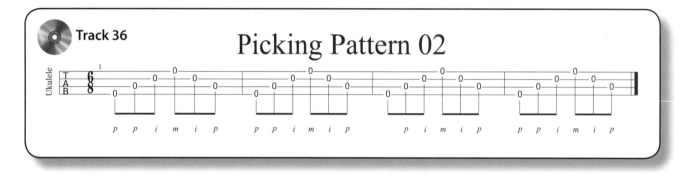

Track 37

Blues It
Picking Pattern 02

Track 38

COUNTING 6/8 TIME

	ONE	Two	Three	FOUR	Five	Six	ONE	Two	Three	FOUR	Five	Six
6/8	1	2	3	4	5	6	1	2	3	4	5	6

MORE FUN PICKIN' PATTERNS

Practice these additional Picking Patterns.

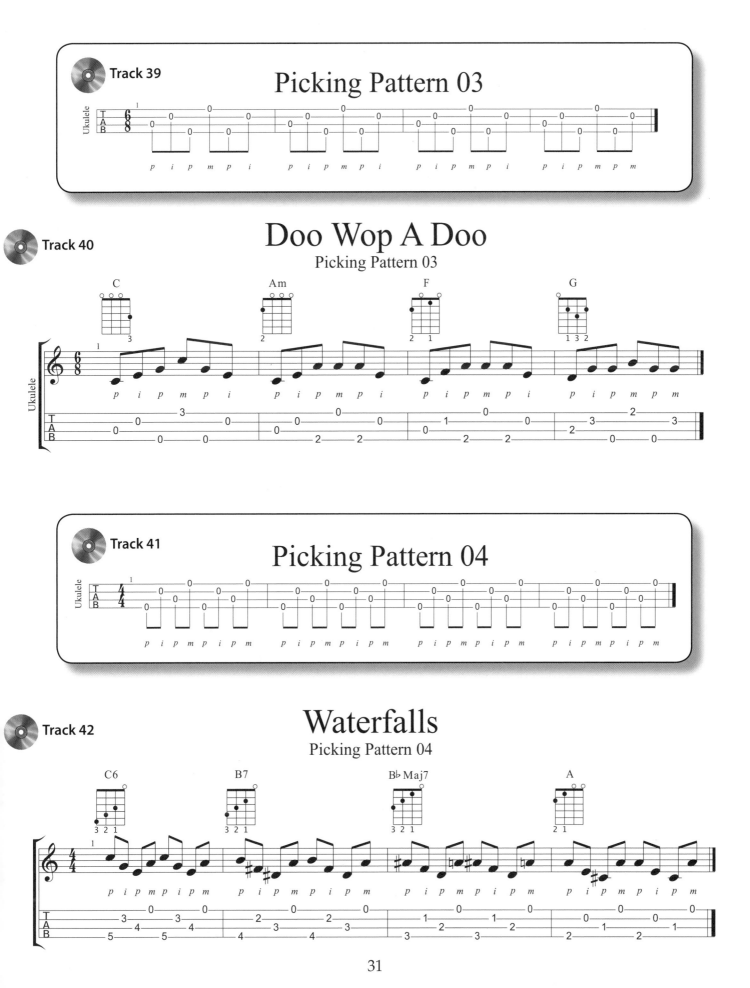

Track 39 — Picking Pattern 03

Track 40 — Doo Wop A Doo
Picking Pattern 03

Track 41 — Picking Pattern 04

Track 42 — Waterfalls
Picking Pattern 04

QuickStart UKE

Stairway
In the style of Led Zeppelin

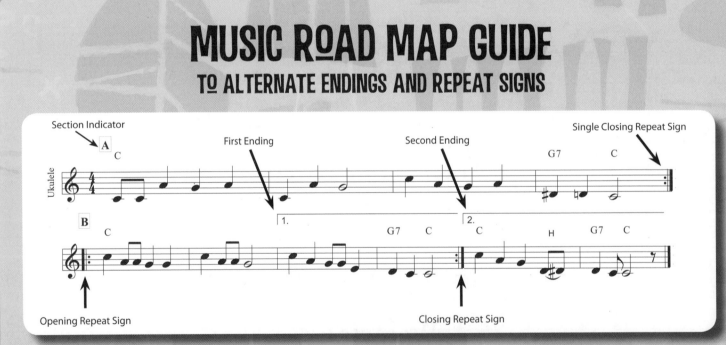

MUSIC ROAD MAP GUIDE
TO ALTERNATE ENDINGS AND REPEAT SIGNS

IF YOU CAN READ THE SIGNS ON A MUSIC ROAD MAP YOU WILL NEVER GET LOST.

The **SINGLE CLOSING REPEAT** tells you to go back to the beginning.

When you pass an **OPENING REPEAT SIGN** you play until you reach the next **CLOSING REPEAT SIGN** and then go back and play from the **OPENING REPEAT SIGN** again.

When you pass the **FIRST ENDING** you play until the **CLOSING REPEAT SIGN** and go back to the nearest **OPENING REPEAT SIGN**. Since we already played the **FIRST ENDING** we take a detour and continue playing the **SECOND ENDING**.

Island Thirds

Music by KEV-Kevin Rones

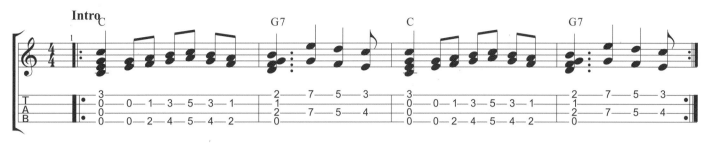

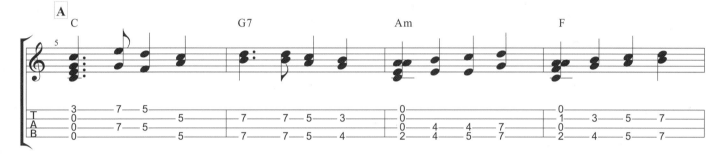

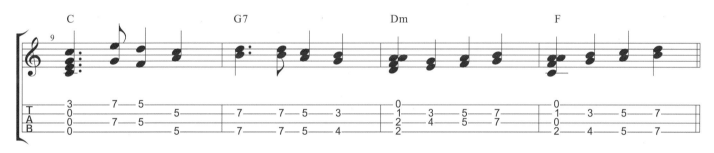

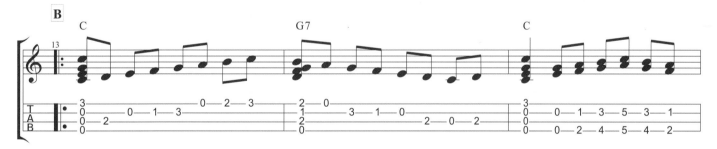

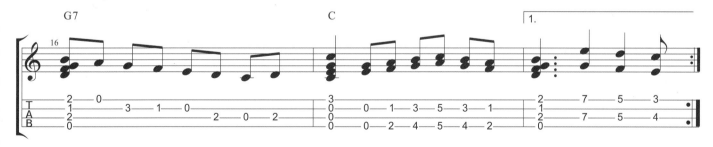

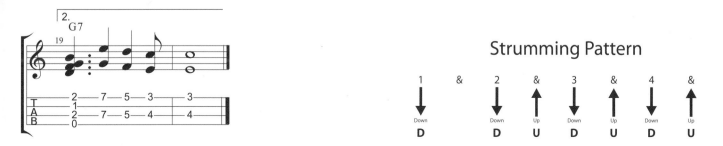

Strumming Pattern

1	&	2	&	3	&	4	&
↓		↓	↑	↓	↑	↓	↑
Down		Down	Up	Down	Up	Down	Up
D		**D**	**U**	**D**	**U**	**D**	**U**

BASIC NOTE READING FOR UKULELE

These are the notes available on most ukuleles. Ukuleles strung with a Low G string have 5 additional notes.

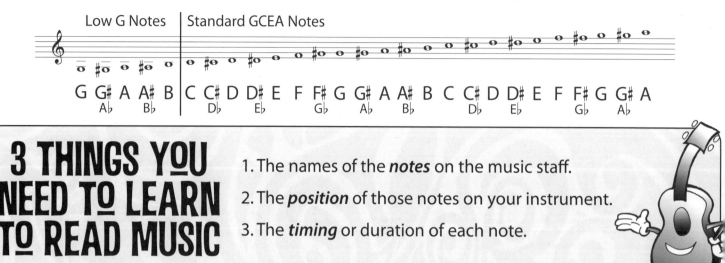

Low G Notes	Standard GCEA Notes

G G# A A# B | C C# D D# E F F# G G# A A# B C C# D D# E F F# G G# A
 A♭ B♭ | D♭ E♭ G♭ A♭ B♭ D♭ E♭ G♭ A♭

3 THINGS YOU NEED TO LEARN TO READ MUSIC

1. The names of the *notes* on the music staff.
2. The *position* of those notes on your instrument.
3. The *timing* or duration of each note.

THE EASY WAY TO REMEMBER THE NAMES OF THE NOTES ON THE STAFF

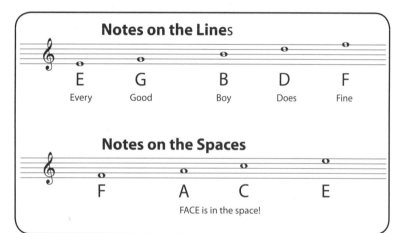

Notes on the Lines

E G B D F
Every Good Boy Does Fine

Notes on the Spaces

F A C E
FACE is in the space!

To remember the notes that fall on the lines of the staff use the mnemonic:

Every Good Boy Does Fine

To remember the names of the notes that fall on spaces use the mnemonic:

F A C E is in the spaces

TIMING IS EVERYTHING. LEARNING NOTE VALUES IS EASY AS PIE!

Quarter note 1 beat	Eighth Note 1/2 beat	Half Note 2 beats	Whole Note 4 beats

Quarter note Rest	Eighth Note Rest	Half note Rest	Whole note Rest

Try using these words to represent simple note values.

Pie	App-le	&	Hot Pie	Pie -2 - 3 - 4

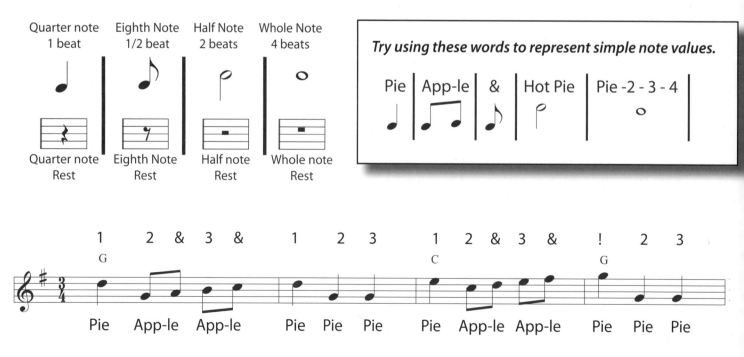

1	2 & 3 &	1	2	3	1	2 & 3 &	!	2	3

Pie App-le App-le Pie Pie Pie Pie App-le App-le Pie Pie Pie

34

LEARNING NOTES ON EACH STRING

Say It & Play It! Play each of these exercises saying the note name as you play it.

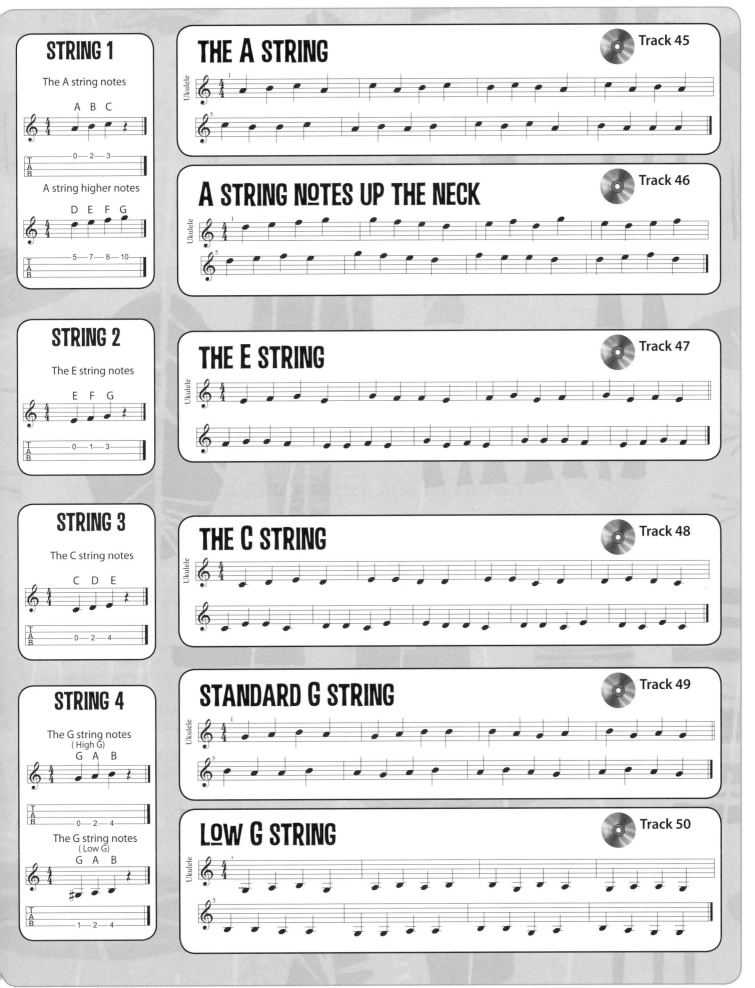

STRING 1

The A string notes

A B C

A string higher notes

D E F G

THE A STRING — Track 45

A STRING NOTES UP THE NECK — Track 46

STRING 2

The E string notes

E F G

THE E STRING — Track 47

STRING 3

The C string notes

C D E

THE C STRING — Track 48

STRING 4

The G string notes
(High G)

G A B

The G string notes
(Low G)

G A B

STANDARD G STRING — Track 49

LOW G STRING — Track 50

THE AMAZING C SCALE

There's more than one way to play a C Scale! Here are two different ways to play the same C Scale!

It's time to read music! Practice sight reading the C scale exercise. Remember to *Say It & Play It*.

Track 52

C Scale Exercise

MORE MUSIC STUFF YOU SHOULD KNOW ABOUT SHARPS, FLATS AND NATURALS

Flight of the Bumblebee

E Note Original Pitch

The *Flat* lowers the **E** note 1/2 step (1 fret) to **Eb**

A *Natural* Cancels the Flat returning the **E** note to its original pitch.

Original **C** note
The Sharp Raises the **C** note 1/2 step (1 fret) to **C#**

The **KEY SIGNATURE** is found at the beginning of a piece of music. *Sharps* or *Flats* found in the *Key Signature* tell us that every note represented by a *Sharp* or *Flat* on a line of the staff is raised or lowered 1/2 step (1 fret) throughout the piece unless otherwise noted.

The KEY OF D has 2 sharps: **F#** and **C#**. All of the notes that fall on any **F** and **C** note throughout the piece would be raised 1/2 step (1 fret).

Sharps, Flats and Naturals are sometimes referred to as **ACCIDENTALS**.

Two notes can have the same name. When this happens they are said to be **ENHARMONIC**.
F# and Gb, or C# and Db are examples of enharmonic equivalents.

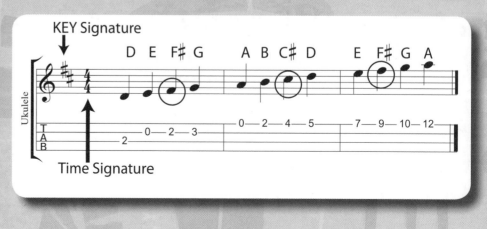

KEY Signature

Time Signature

36

Practice sight reading the following exercises and then listen to the Exersong™ track to see how you did. You can practice strumming your chords and then replay the track and practice the melody notes.

Notes on the Fretboard

Each of the numbers represents a fret on the ukulele.
Use this guide as a reference to identify notes on the fretboard.

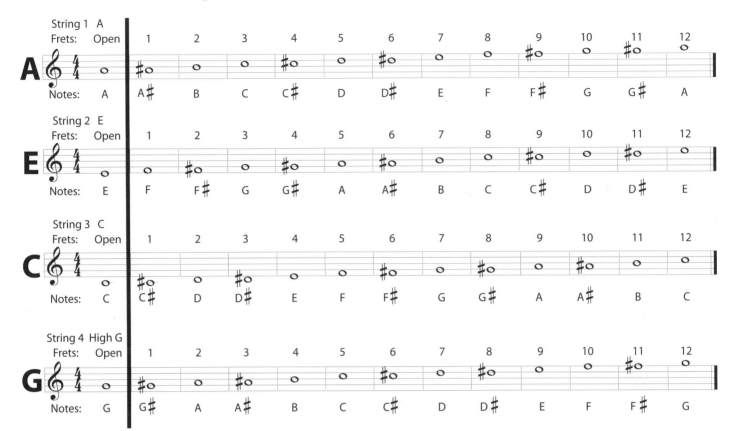

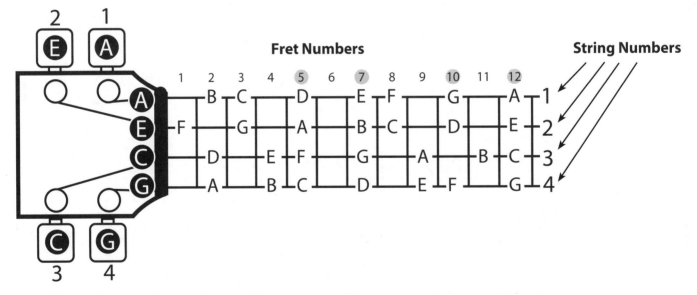

Fret Numbers

String Numbers

Use these notes for C tuning with a low G string

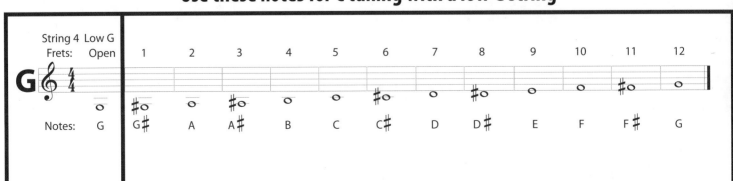

ABOUT THE AUTHOR

KEV– Kevin Rones is a San Diego based author, illustrator, educator and acoustic performer.

His popular KEV's QuickStart™ Workshops for Ukulele and Guitar inspire and educate people everywhere he teaches.

He is the creator of the QuickStart™ Methods for Ukulele and Guitar, founder of the San Diego Guitar Society, The School of Guitar Wizardry™ and The Acoustic Underground™ Concert Series, and a Ukulele Instructor at the San Diego Ukulele Festival.

For information on QuickStart Workshops, QuickStart™ products, KEV performances, On-line lessons or to schedule a KEV Quickstart™ Workshop in your area visit www.KEVmusic.com

WHERE DO YOU GO FROM HERE?

Now that you have a basic understanding of the ukulele and some new ukulele skills it's time to get out there and play! You will find the ukulele community a warm and friendly place filled with really great people. Take some classes, try a workshop, join a ukulele group. Write songs, start a band and remember.... *UKE Can Do it!*

BUY THIS BOOK!

AVAILABLE NOW. ASK FOR IT AT YOUR LOCAL MUSIC STORE.

Wev'e got new QuickStart™ products in the works! Including new online lessons, DVDs and Books. Check www.**KEV**music.com for updates.

SPECIAL THANKS ARE IN ORDER

A special thanks to all the great folks at KALA BRAND MUSIC CO. You're awesome!

Thanks to Rick Carleson & Joy Cafiero for helping me make things happen!

Thanks to all my students and workshop attendees for making what I do so much fun!

Photography: Dakota Rones

Ukulele Model Guy: The amazing Kimo Shim!

Thanks to Bari Zwirn for 11th hour proofing and your continued support on my ukulele adventures!

Thanks to Mick Fritzching for late night last minute CD tracking and for coffee, chips and salsa.

More Great Ukulele Books from Centerstream...

CHRISTMAS UKULELE, HAWAIIAN STYLE

Play your favorite Christmas songs Hawaiian style with expert uke player Chika Nagata. This book/CD pack includes 12 songs, each played 3 times: the first and third time with the melody, the second time without the melody so you can play or sing along with the rhythm-only track. Songs include: Mele Kalikimaka (Merry Christmas to You) • We Wish You a Merry Christmas • Jingle Bells (with Hawaiian lyrics) • Angels We Have Heard on High • Away in a Manger • Deck the Halls • Hark! The Herald Angels Sing • Joy to the World • O Come, All Ye Faithful • Silent Night • Up on the Housetop • We Three Kings.
00000472 Book/CD Pack $19.95

FUN SONGS FOR UKULELE

50 terrific songs in standard notation and tablature for beginning to advanced ukulele players. Includes Hawaiian songs, popular standards, classic Western, Stephen Foster and more, with songs such as: The Darktown Strutters Ball • I'm Always Chasing Rainbows • Hot Lips • Gentle Annie • Maikai Waipio • Whispering • Ja-Da • China Boy • Colorado Trail • and many more. Also includes a chord chart and a special section on how to hold the ukulele.
00000407...$14.95

ULTIMATE LIT'L UKULELE CHORDS, PLUS

by Kahuna Uke (aka Ron Middlebrook)
This handy 6' x 9' guide in the popular C tuning provides all the ukulele chords you'll ever need or use. The diagrams are easy to use and follow, with all the principal chords in major and minor keys, in all the different chords positions. Plus, there are sections on How to Begin, Scales on All Strings, Note Studies, and Chord Modulations (great to use for intros & endings!). This handy 32 page guide fits right in a case perfectly. Happy strumming, you'll Mahalo me latter.
00001351...$7.99

ASAP UKULELE
Learn How to Play the Ukulele Way
by Ron Middlebrook
This easy new method will teach you the ukulele ASAP! Each exercise in the book has been designed to teach you the most popular key chord combinations and patterns that you'll see in hundreds of songs. The tunes taught here include: Auld Lang Syne - My Bonnie Lies Over the Ocean - Oh! Susanna - Peg of My Heart - Red River Valley - Tiger Rag - and many more. You can strum the chords for each, or play the easy-to-follow melody.
00001359...$14.99

KEV'S QUICKSTART FINGERSTYLE UKULELE
by Kevin Rones
Go Beyond Three Chords And A Strum!
This book/CD package is for anyone who want to become better at playing the ukulele.
Newbies: Have fun learning how to play Fingerstyle Ukulele quickly without having to read music! **Ukulele Strummers:** Tired of strumming the same old chords? This book will have you picking in no time! **Indie Artist and Songwriters:** Expand you song writing and performance with Fingerstyle Ukulele. **Guitars players:** If you already play guitar this book is your shortcut into learning Ukulele. Learn arrangements written specifically for Fingerstyle Ukulele: Bach, Blues, Folk, Celtic and more!
000001590...$17.99

UKULELE FOR COWBOYS

40 of your favorite cowboy songs in chords, standard notation and tab. Includes: Buffalo Gals • Night Herding Song • Doney Gal • Old Chisholm Trail • The Big Corral • Ragtime Cowboy Joe • Colorado Trail • Old Paint • Yellow Rose of Texas • Green Grow the Lilacs • and many more. Also includes a chord chart, historical background on many of the songs, and a short story on the history of the Hawaiian Cowboy.
00000408 ....$14.99

UKULELE SONGBOOK

compiled by Ron Middlebrook
This terrific collection for beginning to advanced ukulele players features easy arrangements of 50 great songs, in standard notation and tablature. Also teaches popular strum patterns, and how to tune the uke.
00000248 ....$9.95

UKULELE CHORDS
Plus Intros and Endings
by Ron Middlebrook
This handy chart includes clear, easy-to-see chord fingerings in all keys, plus a bonus section that provides favorite intros and endings in different keys. Also includes information on relative tuning.
00000246 ....$2.95

SONGS OF THE CIVIL WAR FOR UKULELE

by Dick Sheridan
25 tunes of the era that boosted morale, championed causes, pulled on the heartstrings, or gave impetus to battle. Includes: All Quiet Along the Potomac, Aura Lee, Battle Hymn of the Republic, Dixie, The Girl I Left Behind Me, John Brown's Body, When Johnny Comes Marching Home and more - all in standard C tuning, with notation, tablature and accompanying lyrics. The book also includes notes on the songs, historical commentary, and a handy chord chart!
00001588...$14.99

THE LOW G STRING TUNING UKULELE

by Ron Middlebrook
25 popular songs for the ukulele in standard music notation, tablature and easy chords. To get the most out of this book, you'll want to replace the fourth (high G) string with one of a heavier gauge and tune it an octave lower to get that full, deep sound – a lá Hawaiian uke virtuoso Jesse Kalima – in playing the melodies in this book. The chords can be played with or without the low G sound.
00001534 Book/CD Pack $19.99

CENTERSTREAM®

P.O. Box 17878 - Anaheim Hills, CA 92817
(714) 779-9390   www.centerstream-usa.com